Tools

Search

Notes

Discuss

 MyReportLinks.com Books

Go!

PRESIDENTS

WOODROW WILSON

A MyReportLinks.com Book

Henry M. Holden

MyReportLinks.com Books

an imprint of

 Enslow Publishers, Inc. **E**

Box 398, 40 Industrial Road
Berkeley Heights, NJ 07922
USA

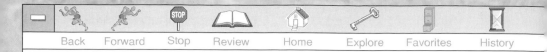

MyReportLinks.com Books, an imprint of Enslow Publishers, Inc. MyReportLinks is a trademark of Enslow Publishers, Inc.

Copyright © 2003 by Enslow Publishers, Inc.

Library of Congress Cataloging-in-Publication Data

Holden, Henry M.
  Woodrow Wilson / Henry M. Holden.
    p. cm. — (Presidents)
Summary: A biography of Woodrow Wilson, who became the twenty-eighth president four years before the nation entered World War I and is known for his plans for peace and a League of Nations.
Includes bibliographical references and index.
  ISBN 0-7660-5123-4
  1. Wilson, Woodrow, 1856–1924—Juvenile literature. 2. Presidents—United States—Biography—Juvenile literature. [1. Wilson, Woodrow, 1856–1924. 2. Presidents.] I. Title. II. Series.
  E767 .H45 2003
  973.91'3'092—dc21

                                    2002007477

Printed in the United States of America

10 9 8 7 6 5 4 3 2 1

To Our Readers:
Through the purchase of this book, you and your library gain access to the Report Links that specifically back up this book.
The Publisher will provide access to the Report Links that back up this book and will keep these Report Links up to date on **www.myreportlinks.com** for three years from the book's first publication date.
We have done our best to make sure all Internet addresses in this book were active and appropriate when we went to press. However, the author and the Publisher have no control over, and assume no liability for, the material available on those Internet sites or on other Web sites they may link to.
The usage of the MyReportLinks.com Books Web site is subject to the terms and conditions stated on the Usage Policy Statement on **www.myreportlinks.com**.
In the future, a password may be required to access the Report Links that back up this book. The password is found on the bottom of page 4 of this book.
Any comments or suggestions can be sent by e-mail to comments@myreportlinks.com or to the address on the back cover.

Photo Credits: © Corel Corporation, pp. 1 (background), 3; Department of the Interior, p. 22; Enslow Publishers, Inc., pp. 14, 16, 17; Library of Congress, pp. 1, 20, 23, 25; MyReportLinks.com Books, p. 4; National Archives and Records Administration, pp. 11, 30, 34, 37; National Trust for Historic Preservation, p. 42; PBS, *American Experience*, pp. 15, 35; The White House, p. 27; University of San Diego, p. 39; Woodrow Wilson Birthplace Foundation, p. 13; Woodrow Wilson House, p. 18.

Cover Photo: © Corel Corporation; Library of Congress.

Contents

About MyReportLinks.com Books

MyReportLinks.com Books
Great Books, Great Links, Great for Research!

MyReportLinks.com Books present the information you need to learn about your report subject. In addition, they show you where to go on the Internet for more information. The pre-evaluated Report Links that back up this book are kept up to date on **www.myreportlinks.com**. With the purchase of a MyReportLinks.com Books title, you and your library gain access to the Report Links that specifically back up that book. The Report Links save hours of research time and link to dozens—even hundreds—of Web sites, source documents, and photos related to your report topic.

Please see "To Our Readers" on the Copyright page for important information about this book, the MyReportLinks.com Books Web site, and the Report Links that back up this book.

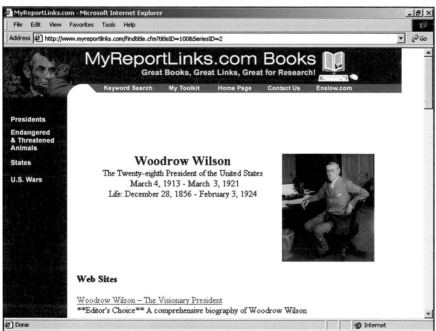

Access:

The Publisher will provide access to the Report Links that back up this book and will try to keep these Report Links up to date on our Web site for three years from the book's first publication date. Please enter **PWW7658** if asked for a password.

Report Links

 The Internet sites described below can be accessed at
http://www.myreportlinks.com

*EDITOR'S CHOICE

▶ **Woodrow Wilson—The Visionary President**
This Web site includes a comprehensive biography of Woodrow
Wilson, a discussion of his impact and legacy as president, and
his life before, during, and after his administrations.

Link to this Internet site from http://www.myreportlinks.com
*EDITOR'S CHOICE

▶ **Woodrow Wilson**
Explore the life and presidential career of Woodrow Wilson through
an interactive time line, images, and narratives. Here you will learn
about his legislative accomplishments, the League of Nations, and
much more.

Link to this Internet site from http://www.myreportlinks.com
*EDITOR'S CHOICE

▶ **Woodrow Wilson: Prophet of Peace**
This Web site describes Wilson's efforts to have the United States join
the League of Nations.

Link to this Internet site from http://www.myreportlinks.com
*EDITOR'S CHOICE

▶ **"I Do Solemnly Swear . . ."**
Experience Woodrow Wilson's inaugurations through memorabilia.
View images of Wilson's first inaugural address in shorthand, an
invitation to the inaugural ceremonies, and other original documents.

Link to this Internet site from http://www.myreportlinks.com
*EDITOR'S CHOICE

▶ **Objects From the Presidency**
At this site you will find objects related to President Woodrow Wilson
and a description of the era he lived in. You will also learn about the
office of the presidency.

Link to this Internet site from http://www.myreportlinks.com
*EDITOR'S CHOICE

▶ **Thomas Woodrow Wilson Was Born December 28, 1856**
America's Story from America's Library, a Library of Congress Web site,
tells the story of Woodrow Wilson and his presidency. Here you will
learn about the difficult decisions he faced during his administration.

Link to this Internet site from http://www.myreportlinks.com

 The Internet sites described below can be accessed at
http://www.myreportlinks.com

▶ **The American Presidency: Woodrow Wilson**
This biography of Woodrow Wilson includes an overview of Wilson's life
from the time of his birth in Staunton, Virginia, in 1856, to his death
in Washington, D.C., in 1924. You will also find a bibliography and
additional links.

Link to this Internet site from http://www.myreportlinks.com

▶ **American Presidents: Life Portraits: Woodrow Wilson**
Here you will find "Life Facts" and "Did you know?" trivia about Woodrow
Wilson. You will also find a letter written by Wilson to his second wife,
Edith Bolling Galt.

Link to this Internet site from http://www.myreportlinks.com

▶ **Board of Governors of the Federal Reserve System**
President Woodrow Wilson created the Federal Reserve System when he
signed the Federal Reserve Act into law on December 23, 1913. The Federal
Reserve's Web site includes information regarding the Federal Reserve's
activities and programs.

Link to this Internet site from http://www.myreportlinks.com

▶ **The First Mother's Day—May 9, 1914**
America's Story from America's Library, a Library of Congress Web site, gives
the history of Mother's Day, first proclaimed by Woodrow Wilson on May 9,
1914, when he asked the American public to thank their mothers.

Link to this Internet site from http://www.myreportlinks.com

▶ **First World War.com**
Much of Wilson's two terms in office was spent in the shadow of the First
World War. This site presents an in-depth overview of the war, providing
unique insights into topics such as chemical warfare and Iraq in World War I.

Link to this Internet site from http://www.myreportlinks.com

▶ **Mr. President: Woodrow Wilson**
Here you will find basic facts about Woodrow Wilson including a quote
and a brief description of his administration.

Link to this Internet site from http://www.myreportlinks.com

The Internet sites described below can be accessed at
http://www.myreportlinks.com

▶ **The 1919 Nobel Peace Prize**
Woodrow Wilson was awarded the 1919 Nobel Peace Prize for his
efforts to end the First World War and bring peace to the world. The
official Web site of the Nobel Foundation offers a biography of Wilson
as well as the text of his acceptance specch.

Link to this Internet site from http://www.myreportlinks.com

▶ **The Presidents of Princeton**
From 1902 to 1910, Woodrow Wilson was the president of Princeton
University, in Princeton, New Jersey. Here you will find a brief
overview of his accomplishments as president of Princeton.

Link to this Internet site from http://www.myreportlinks.com

▶ **President Thomas Woodrow Wilson**
At this Web site you will find a comprehensive list of events that
occurred during Wilson's administration and a list of all of his cabinet
members. Also included are original audio and links to the president's
inaugural addresses.

Link to this Internet site from http://www.myreportlinks.com

▶ **Ten Suffragists Arrested While Picketing at the White House**
America's Story from America's Library, a Library of Congress Web site,
tells the story of the women's suffrage movement and Woodrow
Wilson's reaction to it. You will also learn about Alice Paul and the
hunger strike that led Wilson to support women's suffrage.

Link to this Internet site from http://www.myreportlinks.com

▶ **Today in History**
Woodrow Wilson served two consecutive terms in the White House.
At this Web site you will learn about some of the controversial issues
Wilson faced during his administrations, including the decision to
involve the United States in World War I.

Link to this Internet site from http://www.myreportlinks.com

▶ **The United Nations**
In 1918, Woodrow Wilson called for the creation of a League of Nations.
Although the League of Nations did not last, the United Nations has
lasted. This official Web site includes information about United Nations
programs and activities worldwide.

Link to this Internet site from http://www.myreportlinks.com

▶ **The Versailles Treaty**
Following the end of the First World War, President Wilson was instrumental in negotiating the Treaty of Versailles. This site, managed by the history department at the University of San Diego, includes the full text of the treaty and includes maps, photos, and cartoons.

Link to this Internet site from http://www.myreportlinks.com

▶ **The White House: Edith Bolling Galt Wilson**
The official White House Web site holds the biography of Edith Bolling Galt Wilson. Here you will learn about her life, how she met Woodrow Wilson, and her experiences as First Lady.

Link to this Internet site from http://www.myreportlinks.com

▶ **The White House: Ellen Louise Axson Wilson**
The official White House Web site holds the biography of Ellen Louise Axson Wilson. Here you will learn about her life and experiences in the White House.

Link to this Internet site from http://www.myreportlinks.com

▶ **The White House: Woodrow Wilson**
The official White House Web site holds the biography of Woodrow Wilson. This site includes links to biographies of his two wives, Ellen Louise Axson Wilson and Edith Bolling Galt Wilson.

Link to this Internet site from http://www.myreportlinks.com

▶ **Wilson, Woodrow**
Bartleby.com provides a comprehensive biography of the twenty-eighth president of the United States.

Link to this Internet site from http://www.myreportlinks.com

▶ **The Woodrow Wilson Birthplace—Staunton, Virginia**
At the Woodrow Wilson Birthplace Web site, you can take a virtual tour of Wilson's home and view images of artifacts from his life and times.

Link to this Internet site from http://www.myreportlinks.com

Report Links

The Internet sites described below can be accessed at
http://www.myreportlinks.com

▶**Woodrow Wilson—First Inaugural Address**
This page presents the full text of Woodrow Wilson's first inaugural
address, given on Tuesday, March 4, 1913, on the East Portico of
the Capitol.

Link to this Internet site from http://www.myreportlinks.com

▶**Woodrow Wilson House**
Woodrow Wilson was the first president to establish a permanent
residence in Washington, D.C., and the only president to have a
presidential museum in the nation's capital. At this Web site you can
take a tour of that home, which is a National Historic Landmark.

Link to this Internet site from http://www.myreportlinks.com

▶**Woodrow Wilson—Second Inaugural Address**
This page presents the full text of Woodrow Wilson's second inaugural
address, given on Monday, March 5, 1917. Wilson, elected on the
strength of the slogan "He kept us out of war," asked Congress to
declare war on Germany only one month later.

Link to this Internet site from http://www.myreportlinks.com

▶**Woodrow Wilson's Speech Notes in Shorthand**
In January 1918, President Wilson presented his peace plan to Congress.
The plan came to be known as the "Fourteen Points." At this Library of
Congress site, Wilson's shorthand notes for the Fourteen Points speech
can be seen.

Link to this Internet site from http://www.myreportlinks.com

▶**Woodrow Wilson, Twenty-eighth President of the
United States**
Part of the Internet Public Library, this site presents a variety of
statistics and a collection of information relating to Woodrow Wilson.

Link to this Internet site from http://www.myreportlinks.com

▶**The World War I Document Archive**
This repository of documents relating to World War I includes the
transcript of Wilson's Fourteen Points speech and his April 1917
war message.

Link to this Internet site from http://www.myreportlinks.com

Highlights

1856—*Dec. 28:* Born in Staunton, Virginia.

1879—Graduates from the College of New Jersey (renamed Princeton University in 1896).

1885—*June 24:* Marries Ellen Louise Axson.

1885–1890—Teaches political economy and public law at Bryn Mawr College and history at Wesleyan University.

1890–1902—Is professor of jurisprudence and political economy at College of New Jersey.

1902–1910—Serves as president of Princeton University.

1910—*Nov. 8:* Elected governor of New Jersey.

1912—*Nov. 5:* Elected president of the United States.

1913—*Dec. 23:* Signs Federal Reserve Act, creating the Federal Reserve System.

1914—World War I starts in Europe.

—*Aug. 6:* Wife, Ellen Louise Axson, dies.

1915—*Dec. 18:* Marries Edith Bolling Galt.

1916—*Nov. 7:* Reelected president.

1917—*April 2:* Asks Congress for a declaration of war against Germany.

1918—*Jan. 8:* Announces his Fourteen Points plan for peace in Europe.

1918–1919—June: Leads American delegation to the Paris Peace Conference.

—The Eighteenth Amendment, prohibiting the sale or distribution of alcoholic beverages, is ratified.

1920—The Nineteenth Amendment, extending women the right to vote, is ratified.

—Wilson is awarded the Nobel Peace Prize of 1919, for his efforts to achieve world peace and establish the League of Nations.

1921—*March 3:* Second term ends.

1924—*Feb. 3:* Dies, in Washington, D.C.

Declaration of War

As president of the United States, Woodrow Wilson had managed to keep America from entering the Great War, as World War I was originally called, for three years. He had won a second term on the slogan "He kept us out of war." Wilson hated war and violence, but world events caused him to change course by April 2, 1917.

That spring in Washington, D.C., the cherry trees were in bloom, and the chill of winter was quickly fading

▲ On February 3, 1917, President Wilson appeared before Congress, announcing a break in relations with Germany. Two months later, he would appear before Congress again—to ask them for a declaration of war.

from memory. Escorted by cavalry, Wilson's carriage made its way to the Capitol building.[1] Thousands of people lined the streets, many waving small American flags and cheering the president. For Woodrow Wilson, however, the day was a somber one. As a child growing up during the Civil War, he had seen soldiers afflicted with horrible wounds. Now a world war being waged in Europe by the Allies (Great Britain, France, Italy, and Russia, among other countries) and the Central Powers (Germany, Austria-Hungary, and others) had already taken millions of lives. With German submarines sinking American cargo ships, Wilson was about to ask Congress to declare war on Germany. He had no quarrel with the German people, he said, but rather with Germany's "irresponsible government."[2] Wilson knew that as commander in chief of the United States armed forces, he would be sending thousands of Americans to their deaths overseas.

Wilson addressed Congress and asked for a declaration of war against Germany, saying, "We have no selfish end to serve. We desire no conquest, no domination. We seek . . . no material compensation for the sacrifice we shall freely make . . . Neutrality is no longer feasible or desirable. . . ."[3]

Congress listened, debated the issue, and then voted on April 6, 1917, to declare war on Germany. In two months' time, American troops would begin their 3,000-mile trip across the Atlantic Ocean—to make the world, in Wilson's words, "safe for democracy."[4]

Growing Up, 1856–1890

Thomas Woodrow Wilson was born on December 28, 1856, in Staunton, Virginia, to Jessie Woodrow Wilson and Joseph Ruggles Wilson. He had two sisters, Marion and Anne, and a brother, Joseph, Jr. Young Thomas, who would later be known by his middle name, was the son, grandson, and nephew of Presbyterian ministers. The Bible played an important role in his life. He would develop a

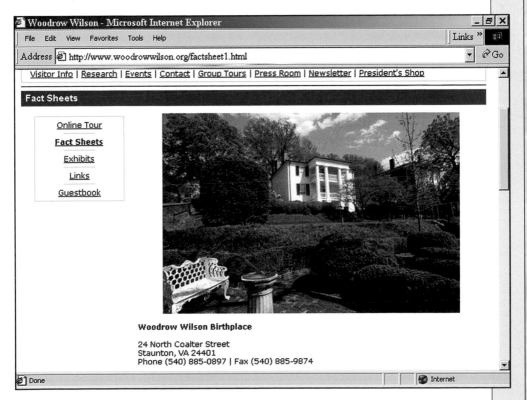

Thomas Woodrow Wilson was born in this home in Staunton, Virginia, on December 28, 1856.

The Reverend Dr. Joseph Ruggles Wilson, Woodrow Wilson's father.

life-long habit of reading from it before bed.[1]

Thomas's family moved to Augusta, Georgia, when he was about two years old. His father had become pastor of a Presbyterian church there. "My earliest recollection," Wilson later said, "is of standing at my father's gateway . . . when I was four years old, and hearing someone pass and say that Mr. Lincoln was elected and there was to be war."[2] Less than a year later, the Civil War began. His father, a Southerner and a supporter of the Confederacy, opened his church as a hospital for wounded soldiers. The church graveyard served as a stockade for Union prisoners.[3] Wilson later recalled seeing badly wounded soldiers treated in the church.[4]

When Thomas Wilson was eight years old, Jefferson Davis, the president of the Confederate States of America, passed through Augusta. Thomas and others watched as Yankee soldiers took Davis to prison.[5] The Civil War and its aftermath would have a lasting impact on Woodrow Wilson.

▶ Trying Times at School

Young Thomas Wilson was almost ten years old before letters began making sense to him. He had the learning disorder called dyslexia, which made reading and writing difficult.

With few friends, Thomas Wilson formed a close bond with his strict but loving father, who often read to him and taught him how to become a great speaker. He would make young Thomas Wilson practice the speeches of great men.

At the age of sixteen, Thomas learned shorthand, a method of substituting symbols or abbreviations for words that allows a writer to write quickly. With this new skill, he was able to take better notes, and his grades improved. In later life, he used shorthand to write most of his speeches.[6]

After graduating from high school, Wilson thought of becoming a minister. In 1874, he enrolled at Davidson College in North Carolina to study for the ministry. While

PBS - American Experience: Woodrow Wilson | Gallery - Microsoft Internet Explorer

File   Edit   View   Favorites   Tools   Help

Links »

Address http://www.pbs.org/wgbh/amex/wilson/gallery/wphotos.html   Go

WOODROW WILSON

THE FILM & MORE
TIMELINE
WILSON-A PORTRAIT
SPECIAL FEATURES
PEOPLE
GALLERY
  Wilson Photo Album
  Poster Art of World War I
TEACHER'S GUIDE

GALLERY | WILSON PHOTO ALBUM

Princeton University

<<   >>

Gallery: Wilson Photo Album | Poster Art of World War I

Done   Internet

▲ In 1879, Woodrow Wilson graduated from the College of New Jersey, later renamed Princeton University.

Jessie Woodrow Wilson, Woodrow Wilson's mother. As an adult, Wilson dropped "Thomas" and called himself "Woodrow," his mother's maiden name.

there, he became a member of the school's debating team and found that he could influence people with words. Through debating, he also learned that he liked politics. But he struggled with schoolwork, and when his health began to suffer, he left school and returned home.

College Days

In 1875, Wilson enrolled in the College of New Jersey (renamed Princeton University in 1896) to study politics. Again, he found schoolwork hard, but this time he did not give up. He joined the debating team and later became the editor of the college newspaper.

Wilson graduated in 1879. He then studied law for a year at the University of Virginia. Although he failed to graduate, he passed the bar exam and began practicing law in Atlanta, Georgia, for a year. Around this time, he dropped his first name, Thomas, and began referring to himself as Woodrow, his middle name and his mother's maiden name.[7]

Marriage and Teaching

In 1883, Wilson abandoned his law practice and entered graduate school at Johns Hopkins University, in Baltimore,

Maryland, to study history and political science—two subjects that would occupy him for the rest of his life. That year, Woodrow Wilson also met Ellen Louise Axson, a young woman from Rome, Georgia. Like Wilson, she was the child of a Presbyterian minister. The two fell in love and were married in June 1885. Woodrow and Ellen Wilson would have three daughters, Margaret, Jessie, and Eleanor.

In 1886, Wilson finished graduate school, earning a Ph.D. in political science from Johns Hopkins. In *Congressional Government*, his doctoral dissertation, he claimed there was little leadership in Congress. He also stated that the presidency, as an institution, was weak and needed to be made stronger.[8] He would work toward that for the rest of his life.

From 1885 to 1888, Wilson taught history and politics at Bryn Mawr College, in Pennsylvania, but he was not happy there. In 1888 he took a job teaching history at Wesleyan University, in Connecticut. In 1890, he left Wesleyan to became a professor of law at the College of New Jersey.

Woodrow Wilson met Ellen Louise Axson in 1883, the year this photograph was taken. The couple married two years later.

From Princeton to the White House, 1890–1913

At the College of New Jersey, Woodrow Wilson became a leading voice on campus. He spoke out on behalf of economic reforms and called for the federal government to be granted new powers to regulate big business. Wilson was a popular figure on campus. For seven of the twelve years he taught there, the students voted him their favorite professor.

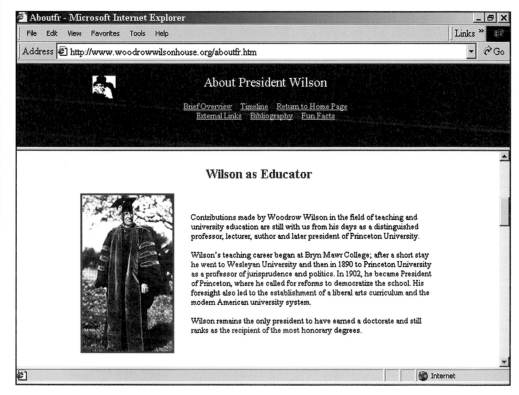

Aboutfr - Microsoft Internet Explorer

File   Edit   View   Favorites   Tools   Help   Links »

Address http://www.woodrowwilsonhouse.org/aboutfr.htm   Go

About President Wilson

Brief Overview   Timeline   Return to Home Page
External Links   Bibliography   Fun Facts

Wilson as Educator

Contributions made by Woodrow Wilson in the field of teaching and university education are still with us from his days as a distinguished professor, lecturer, author and later president of Princeton University.

Wilson's teaching career began at Bryn Mawr College; after a short stay he went to Wesleyan University and then in 1890 to Princeton University as a professor of jurisprudence and politics. In 1902, he became President of Princeton, where he called for reforms to democratize the school. His foresight also led to the establishment of a liberal arts curriculum and the modern American university system.

Wilson remains the only president to have earned a doctorate and still ranks as the recipient of the most honorary degrees.

Internet

▲ *Woodrow Wilson was the first man named president of Princeton University who was not a member of the clergy. His tenure as university president lasted eight years.*

In June 1902, at the age of forty-six, Woodrow Wilson was named president of the now-renamed Princeton University. He was the first layperson to hold that office.

Reforms at Princeton

As the university's president, Wilson could make changes he felt would help the students. He had new classrooms built, hired more teachers, and decreased the size of classes so that students were encouraged to ask questions during lectures.

One of Wilson's reforms that did not work, though, was his plan to close down the university's eating clubs for upperclassmen. These clubs had long been the center of college activity, but Wilson felt they discriminated against poorer students. Wilson tried to introduce a common dining hall, where all students and professors would eat together. But the students and many faculty rebelled, and the eating clubs remained.

Overwork Takes a Toll

At Princeton, Woodrow Wilson worked hard to accomplish his goals for the university, but that hard work soon took its toll. One morning, in 1906, Wilson woke up and realized he could not see out of his left eye. Afterward, doctors diagnosed a broken blood vessel, caused by high blood pressure, and they thought Wilson had probably suffered a mild stroke. The only known "cure" at the time was rest and retirement. Wilson was encouraged to do both, at only forty-nine years of age.

The Wilsons took a brief vacation in England, where he regained some of his sight. He rested, but he would not retire. He returned to Princeton and continued to press for more social reforms.

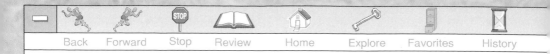
Woodrow Wilson's continued support for reforms got him noticed by the Democratic Party in New Jersey. In 1910 the Democrats asked him to run for governor of New Jersey. Wilson saw the campaign as a chance to spread his ideas for reform to a wider audience. His was a fresh, new voice on the political scene, and he won the New Jersey gubernatorial election in a landslide.

▶ Governor of New Jersey

As governor, Wilson brought significant economic reform to New Jersey. He signed bills to stop corruption and to reduce the powers of corporations. He also got a law passed that created party primaries in which citizens rather than

▲ Family portrait: Woodrow and Ellen Wilson and their daughters, in 1912.

the state legislature elected all state officials. The old system had led to candidates being elected by a small group of people within a party, and those people were often granted favors for their support.

Wilson signed a law that created a public service commission. This group set the prices that utilities and railroads could charge their customers. He also passed the state's first workers' compensation law, which created a fund for injured workers. These reforms brought Woodrow Wilson national attention, and a Wilson-for-president movement soon began. He toured the country, making speeches for economic reforms, and he was greeted warmly everywhere. After the tour, Wilson decided to seek the Democratic presidential nomination.

▶ A Fight for the Nomination

Wilson didn't have an easy time winning his party's nomination, however. The progressive Democrats, who shared Wilson's desire for reform, were divided between supporting Wilson and James "Champ" Clark, the Speaker of the House of Representatives. When Clark could not get the needed majority of votes for the nomination, the Democrats turned to William Jennings Bryan, an influential member of the party. A former presidential candidate himself, Bryan gave his votes to Wilson, and Woodrow Wilson became the Democratic nominee on the forty-sixth ballot.[1]

▶ 1912 Election

The presidential election of 1912 would decide whether the Progressive movement's curbs on big business, begun by Theodore Roosevelt during his presidency, would continue with Woodrow Wilson. Running against Wilson,

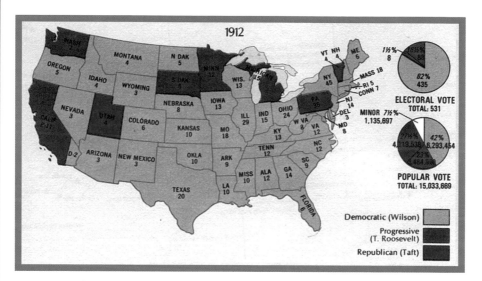

1912

WASH 7

OREGON 5

MONTANA 4

N DAK 5

MINN 12

WIS 13

MICHIGAN 15

VT 4   NH 4   ME 6

IDAHO 4

WYOMING 3

S DAK 5

NEBRASKA 8

IOWA 13

NY 45

MASS 18
RI 5
CONN 7

NEVADA 3

UTAH 4

COLORADO 6

KANSAS 10

ILL 29

IND 15

OHIO 24

PA 38

NJ 14
DEL 3
MD 8

CAL 13

KY 13

W VA 8

VA 12

MO 18

ARIZONA 3

NEW MEXICO 3

OKLA 10

ARK 9

TENN 12

NC 12

D-2

MISS 10

ALA 12

GA 14

SC 9

TEXAS 20

LA 10

FLORIDA 6

1½% 8   16½% 88

82% 435

ELECTORAL VOTE
TOTAL: 531

MINOR 7½% 1,135,697

27½% 4,119,538

42% 6,293,454

23% 4,484,980

POPULAR VOTE
TOTAL: 15,033,669

Democratic (Wilson)
Progressive (T. Roosevelt)
Republican (Taft)

▲ *With the Republican vote split between Taft and Roosevelt, Woodrow Wilson won 435 of 531 electoral votes in the presidential election of 1912.*

the Democratic nominee, were three other candidates. The current president, William Howard Taft, was seen as favoring the interests of big business. The Socialist Party candidate, Eugene V. Debs, believed all workers should have control over the industrial economy.[2] And former Republican president Theodore Roosevelt entered the race as the candidate of the Progressive, or Bull Moose, Party.

It was a lively campaign, with Wilson and Roosevelt touring the country, making speeches, while Taft for the most part stayed in Washington. But with the Republican vote split between Taft and Roosevelt, Wilson was able to win 435 of the 531 electoral votes. Roosevelt got eighty-eight votes, and Taft received eight. Debs received none. In 1912, Woodrow Wilson became the first Southerner elected president since the Civil War. Thomas Riley Marshall of Indiana became his vice president.

Chapter 4 ▶

Wilson's First Administration, 1913–1917

When Woodrow Wilson took office on March 4, 1913, the United States was a country in which crowded cities and industrialization had led to both poverty and the abuse of workers. These conditions existed despite the reforms begun under the Roosevelt and Taft administrations. Wilson saw the need to continue their reforms and go beyond. He began by holding the first presidential press conference, on March 22.[1] Wilson also became the first president since John Adams to address both houses of Congress in person. In the past, presidents had sent

▲ President-elect Wilson shares a laugh with outgoing president Taft at the White House on the day of Wilson's first inauguration, March 4, 1913.

messengers to Congress.[2] One of Wilson's first acts was to ask Congress to pass his tariff bill, called the Underwood Act. It was part of his "New Freedom," a series of reforms that had been the platform of his campaign.

New Freedom

The New Freedom reforms called for wide social and economic changes. Since the Democrats controlled both houses of Congress, Wilson was able to get many of his programs passed.

"Direct democracy" had been a major issue in the 1912 campaign. At the time, the lawmakers in each state elected the members of the United States Senate. Wilson wanted the voters of each state to choose their U.S. senators in direct elections.[3] In 1913, with the passage of the Seventeenth Amendment to the Constitution, those voters gained the right to elect their senators.

In October of that year, Wilson signed into law the Underwood Tariff Act, which lowered tariffs, or taxes, on many imported goods. Wilson believed that high tariffs created monopolies, which were good for big business but bad for the American people.[4] The law was designed to increase trade and reduce prices on some goods. To make up for lost revenue, the act created a graduated federal income tax, the first income tax levied on the American people since the Civil War.

The Establishment of the "Fed"

In December 1913, Wilson signed the Federal Reserve Act, creating the Federal Reserve System. This was considered his most important domestic action. The act set the rules for regulating the nation's banks and provided the country with a safer and more stable money supply.

Through it, twelve Federal Reserve banks were established and a Federal Reserve Board of Governors was named. The Federal Reserve Board was given the power to adjust interest rates on the money people borrowed. In recessions, when unemployment was high and the economy weak, interest rates could be lowered so that people and businesses could afford to borrow money.

The First Lady's Reforms

While Woodrow Wilson was busy with his reforms, Ellen Wilson saw things closer to home that needed changing.

Thomas Woodrow Wilson Was Born - Microsoft Internet Explorer

File   Edit   View   Favorites   Tools   Help   Links »

Address http://www.americaslibrary.gov/pages/jb_1228_wilson_2_e.html   Go

Official program of the Woman Suffrage Parade that tried to overshadow Wilson's inauguration in 1913

Done   Internet

▲ The Women's Suffrage movement staged a parade the day before Wilson's inauguration to bring attention to their cause—the right of women to vote.

She worked to improve housing conditions for African Americans who lived in Washington, D.C. She took members of Congress to areas not far from the White House and showed them houses without heat or indoor plumbing. In time, Congress provided money to have the houses torn down and build new ones.

As First Lady, Ellen Wilson hosted many events at the White House. But she did not seem to have the strength for her new public life, and her health began to fail quickly.[5] By the summer of 1914, President Wilson was spending hours by her bedside. On August 6, with her family around her bed, and Woodrow Wilson holding her hand, Ellen Wilson died of Bright's disease, a kidney ailment.

Wilson mourned her loss for months. He wrote a friend and said he felt "dead in heart and body. . . ."[6]

▶ Continued Crusade for Reform

Despite his grief, Wilson was able to carry on his plans for reform with the Clayton Antitrust Act. The act made it illegal for any business to control the supply or the price of a product. It also held the corporate officers of a company responsible for any illegal business dealings by the company. Further, the act protected the rights of union members to protest unfair labor practices by striking, or refusing to work, until conditions changed.

In September 1914, Wilson signed the Federal Trade Commission Act, which protected small companies from big corporations. Before the act, a large corporation could lower its price on an item so much that smaller companies, who could not afford to lower their prices, would be forced out of business. Without competition, the corporation could then raise the price on that item again. The act made such practices illegal. At the time, it was a big victory for Wilson, and it created new controls on big business. The United States Supreme Court, the highest court of law in the land, would later rule to limit the Federal Trade Commission's power, however.

Wilson continued to make good on his campaign promises. He knew that millions of children worked long hours in dangerous factories, and he wanted to put an end to that. In 1916 he signed the Keating-Owen Act. This law made it illegal to ship goods made by children across state lines. Later, however, the Supreme Court ruled this law unconstitutional.

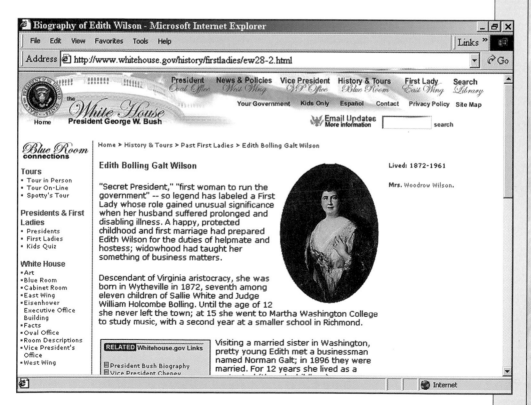

▲ Edith Bolling Galt was descended from Virginia's aristocracy. She became Mrs. Woodrow Wilson on December 18, 1915.

Second Marriage—Edith Bolling Galt

In March 1915, through a chance meeting at the White House, Wilson met Mrs. Edith Bolling Galt, a widow, and the two fell in love. A descendant of the Virginia upper class, whose great-grandmother was Pocahontas, Edith was the seventh of eleven children.

Woodrow Wilson proposed to Edith Galt only two months after meeting her, but they kept their engagement a secret until October. When it was announced, rumors quickly spread. Many people didn't think enough time had passed since Wilson's first wife died. Even though Woodrow Wilson was warned that his relationship with Edith Galt might hurt his chances to be reelected, the two married on December 18, 1915, at her home.

The Brandeis Nomination Battle

In 1916, Wilson chose Louis D. Brandeis as his nominee for the Supreme Court. Brandeis had helped Wilson develop his New Freedom platform. But his politics were considered even more progressive than Wilson's. The *Wall Street Journal* called Brandeis a "rabid . . . super-extreme . . . anti-corporation agitator."[7] And he was the victim of even more personal attacks in the press, including some that were anti-Semitic (against Jews).[8] Wilson, however, stuck by Brandeis. In a close vote, Louis D. Brandeis became the first Jew appointed to serve on the Supreme Court.

Limits to New Freedom

But for some people, Wilson's New Freedom reforms did not go far enough. Poor people were still poor and had little hope. And minorities were still treated unfairly.

In Woodrow Wilson's bid for the presidency, he had won a large African American vote. But once in office, Wilson, a Southerner, often sided with Southern Democrats, who favored segregation, the separation of races. One critic expressed his dismay by asserting "President Wilson has turned his back on the brother in black and has diplomatically closed the political door of hope against him."[9]

Furthermore, during Wilson's first term, the House of Representatives passed a law making interracial marriage a crime in the District of Columbia. And the office of Wilson's postmaster general was segregated, as were other government offices.

▶ Trouble With Mexico

In foreign affairs, Wilson first faced problems close to home. In a 1913 revolution in Mexico, Victoriano Huerta had seized power by arranging for the murder of the former Mexican president, and Wilson would not recognize Huerta or his new government. In April 1914, when Mexican police arrested some American sailors in Tampico, U.S. relations with Mexico deteriorated even more. Wilson sent U.S. Marines to occupy the Mexican city of Veracruz. About ninety Marines and three hundred Mexican soldiers died in a battle, but an all-out war was avoided, and Huerta was finally forced from power.

But even with Huerta gone, Wilson faced a new enemy in Mexico: Francisco "Pancho" Villa, a revolutionary who opposed Venustiano Carranza, Huerta's successor whom the U.S. government recognized. On March 9, 1916, some of Villa's men crossed the border and killed some Americans in New Mexico. Wilson responded by sending an army of some six thousand men, led by General John J. Pershing,

▲ *Francisco "Pancho" Villa (fourth from left), a Mexican revolutionary, was pursued but not captured by General John Pershing and his troops.*

into Mexico. Even though they moved hundreds of miles into Mexico, they were not able to capture Villa. Soon Wilson would be faced with a much greater challenge.

▶ The Great War Begins

In 1913, when Wilson took office, Europe was on the brink of war. Rivalries that had begun in the nineteenth century between Great Britain, France, Germany, and Austria-Hungary had reached the boiling point. An increase in nationalism and imperialism led those countries to expand their armies to protect themselves and their interests. Alliances were then formed between groups of countries. The Triple Alliance consisted of Germany, Italy, and Austria-Hungary. The other alliance, called the Triple Entente, consisted of Great Britain, France, and Russia.

On June 28, 1914, a Serbian nationalist named Gavrilo Princip shot and killed Austrian archduke Francis Ferdinand, the heir to the throne of Austria-Hungary, and his wife. On July 28, Austria-Hungary declared war on Serbia, and Russia came to the aid of Serbia. Germany then declared war on Russia, and France came to the aid of Russia. Germany then declared war on France, and England finally declared war on Germany. The combatants, then, became known as the Allies (Great Britain, France, Russia, and later Italy) and the Central Powers (Germany and Austria-Hungary). Within days, all of Europe was at war.

The United States and Neutrality

The United States, which had strong ties to Great Britain, nevertheless remained neutral for the first three years of the war. Wilson saw his role as a peace broker.[10] And many Americans favored a policy of isolationism—a lack of involvement in foreign affairs. The war was, after all, thousands of miles away. But events gradually led to a change in American sentiment and in Wilson's foreign policy.

On May 7, 1915, a German U-boat, a submarine, torpedoed the *Lusitania*, a large British passenger ship, which had been sailing off the Irish coast. About twelve hundred people died, and among them were more than one hundred Americans. The American public and government were outraged at Germany, but Wilson refrained from sending America to war. Less than a year later, in March 1916, a German U-boat sank an American cargo ship. Wilson issued a harsh warning to Germany, and Germany agreed to stop its submarine attacks. But many Americans suspected that the United States would, sooner or later, be drawn into the war.

Chapter 5

Wilson's Second Administration, 1917–1921

During Wilson's first term as president, his greatest challenge had been keeping America out of the war in Europe. In his reelection campaign, he had promised that the United States would remain neutral. That promise helped him win reelection on November 7, 1916. He defeated his Republican opponent, Charles Evans Hughes, who had been the governor of New York and a Supreme Court justice, in a close contest.

In January 1917, Germany announced it would resume attacks on any ships trading with the Allies. Woodrow Wilson's response a month later was to break off relations with Germany. Then Wilson found out about the Zimmerman telegram.

▶ The Zimmerman Telegram

The British had intercepted and deciphered a coded telegram sent by Arthur Zimmerman, the German foreign minister, to the German minister to Mexico. In it, Zimmerman directed the minister to offer Mexico part of the United States—specifically, Texas, New Mexico, and Arizona—if Mexico agreed to side with Germany in the war. No single message had ever had such an impact on public opinion.[1] It pushed America to the brink of war.

In February, German U-boats sank two American cargo ships. Wilson asked Congress to allow cargo ships to be armed to defend themselves, if attacked—a practice he called "armed neutrality."[2]

On March 5, 1917, Wilson was sworn into office, beginning his second term as president. Two weeks later, German U-boats sank three more unarmed American ships within twenty-four hours. Newspapers labeled the sinkings "an act of war."[3] Wilson met with the members of his cabinet, and they all agreed that a decision must be made.

War Is Declared

On April 2, 1917, Woodrow Wilson appeared before the members of Congress and asked them to declare war on Germany, saying, "The world must be made safe for democracy."[4] On April 6, the United States declared war on Germany. Although most people supported the decision, the country was far from ready for war.

Military Buildup—The War Effort at Home

In 1917 the United States did not have a large enough army to send into battle. In May, Congress passed the Selective Service Act. It gave the government the power to draft men between the age of twenty-one and thirty into the military. About 4 million men were drafted. Almost half of those drafted saw combat duty.[5]

To produce all the things needed to fight the war, factories were open around the clock. Americans bought war bonds, built warships, and rationed food. Congress gave President Wilson wide powers over production. He placed the war industries and railroads under federal control. Wilson also put Herbert Hoover in charge of the Food Administration, a program that asked Americans to consume less of those things that would be needed for the soldiers fighting overseas. Hoover asked the American people to observe "meatless Mondays" and "wheatless Wednesdays." The First Lady contributed to the war effort

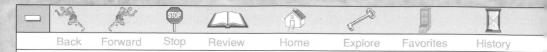

▲ *American women were responsible for much of the production of war materials, including the ordnance made in this Pennsylvania factory in 1918.*

by using sheep to graze on the White House lawn, freeing up gardeners to be drafted into the military. She then auctioned off the sheep's wool and donated the proceeds to the Red Cross.

▶ A Loss of Some Freedoms

During the years that the United States was involved in World War I, Americans came together to support the war effort. But not all Americans were in favor of America's involvement, and many Americans lost some personal freedoms during that time. The post office censored the mail, banning all Socialist newspapers from delivery. President Wilson called for the censorship of news about the war that appeared in the newspapers. Congress, however, refused to pass a censorship law.

On June 15, 1917, Congress did pass an Espionage Act. It imposed a $10,000 fine and twenty-year jail term for anyone who opposed the draft. It also punished people who made comments considered disloyal to America's involvement in the war. A year later the Sedition Act of 1918 went even further, punishing people who did anything to harm the war effort.

To convince Americans that the war was a just cause, a Committee on Public Information was set up. But in practice, it spread fear and distrust, which led to discrimination

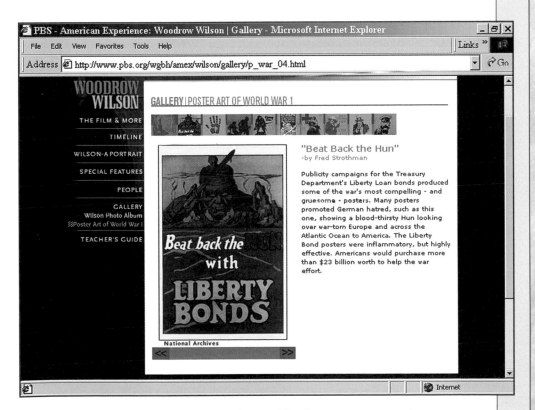

PBS - American Experience: Woodrow Wilson | Gallery - Microsoft Internet Explorer

File   Edit   View   Favorites   Tools   Help

Links »

Address http://www.pbs.org/wgbh/amex/wilson/gallery/p_war_04.html

WOODROW WILSON

GALLERY | POSTER ART OF WORLD WAR 1

THE FILM & MORE
TIMELINE
WILSON-A PORTRAIT
SPECIAL FEATURES
PEOPLE
GALLERY
Wilson Photo Album
Poster Art of World War I
TEACHER'S GUIDE

"Beat Back the Hun"
-by Fred Strothman

Publicity campaigns for the Treasury Department's Liberty Loan bonds produced some of the war's most compelling - and gruesome - posters. Many posters promoted German hatred, such as this one, showing a blood-thirsty Hun looking over war-torn Europe and across the Atlantic Ocean to America. The Liberty Bond posters were inflammatory, but highly effective. Americans would purchase more than $23 billion worth to help the war effort.

Beat back the HUN with LIBERTY BONDS

National Archives

<<   >>

Internet

▲ Posters like this one were designed by the government to play upon the anti-German sentiments of many Americans during the war.

against German Americans and all things German. Movies and pamphlets portrayed Germans as evil, libraries publicly burned German books, schools dropped German courses from their curricula, and some cities even banned public performances of the music of Bach and Beethoven.[6]

▶ Victory in Europe

World War I had raged on for almost four years by the time American troops arrived in Europe in June 1917. Neither the Allies nor the Central Powers was winning. Eighteen months later, with the help of the Americans, the Allies could finally claim victory. On November 11, 1918, Germany signed the armistice that led to the end of the fighting. The war was over. The American troops came home to victory parades. More than one hundred thousand Americans did not return, however. Whether during combat or from accident or disease, they had died fighting for peace in Europe.[7] But by the end of World War I, the United States had become the strongest military power in the world.

▶ The Fourteen Points

Before the war's end, Woodrow Wilson had begun to think about how a lasting peace in Europe could be achieved. He had sent Americans into a war that killed millions of people. He wanted to make sure that a war on that scale would never happen again. On January 8, 1918, Wilson gave a speech before Congress in which he outlined his peace plan, which became known as the Fourteen Points. The plan was to be the standard by which peace came to Europe. Some of the points dealt with general principles by which peace might be maintained: each nation's right to self-determination; open agreements between countries so

War on the western front: A Marine receiving aid before being taken to a hospital, in the Toulon Sector, France, March 22, 1918.

that there were no secret treaties; freedom of the seas; removal of trade barriers; arms reductions; and free and unbiased adjustments to colonial claims. Other points dealt with more specific and immediate concerns brought about by the war. The last point called for the establishment of a League of Nations. Wilson believed a new world organization such as the League, in which each member country was responsible for every other member country, was the way to prevent future wars. Less than ten months after Wilson delivered his speech, he was instrumental in negotiating the armistice that brought an end to World War I.

The League of Nations

As the chief architect of the League of Nations, Wilson envisioned an international association of nations that would band together to protect member nations from attacks. Rather than resorting to war, countries in the League would settle their differences in a court, peacefully.

Following the armistice, Wilson believed he could persuade the leaders of Europe to accept his plan. Edith Wilson urged her husband to attend the Paris Peace Conference, which was being held by the Allied victors to

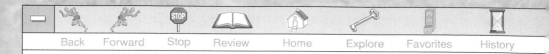
agree on the terms of Germany's surrender. In December 1918, Wilson traveled to Paris with Edith and several close advisors. He was the first sitting president to travel to Europe and the first chief executive to negotiate a treaty while president.

▶ The Paris Peace Conference

At the conference, Wilson met with the heads of twenty-seven nations to share his peace plan, based on his Fourteen Points. But many of the leaders of the countries involved in the war did not embrace all of Wilson's ideas. They had suffered more than America had, they wanted to keep their armies intact, and they wanted to punish Germany for starting the war.

▶ The Big Four and the Treaty of Versailles

The final treaty of the conference came down to an agreement between Wilson, Prime Minister David Lloyd George of Great Britain, Premier Georges Clemenceau of France, and Premier Vittorio Orlando of Italy. These heads of state became known as the Big Four. By the time the conference ended in June 1919, Germany signed the final treaty, the Treaty of Versailles, which was greatly influenced by Wilson's Fourteen Points. But that treaty left Germany with a huge war debt and almost no means to rebuild its country. The treaty also made Germany pay reparations (money settlements) to the Allies to cover the costs of the war. Germany's military was also nearly completely dismantled. And the treaty's harsh terms almost certainly contributed to a rise of nationalism in Germany, which in turn led to the rise of Adolph Hitler, and eventually to the Second World War.

▲ *The Big Four at the Paris Peace Conference: left to right, British prime minister David Lloyd George, Italian premier Vittorio Orlando, French premier Georges Clemenceau, and the American president Woodrow Wilson.*

▶ United States Opposition

While Wilson was in Europe, the Republicans had won seats in Congress and now controlled the Senate. They did not like the Treaty of Versailles or the League of Nations, which would have involved the United States more than ever in world affairs. Furthermore, Wilson had made a mistake by not including any Republicans in the United States delegation to the Paris Peace Conference.

So to rally support for the League, Wilson and his wife began a grueling cross-country trip on September 2, 1919,

of more than eight thousand miles. The trip simply wore the president out, and he began to suffer from sleeplessness and headaches. After giving a speech in Pueblo, Colorado, Wilson collapsed.

A week later, on October 2, Woodrow Wilson suffered a massive stroke. A blood clot burst in an artery of Wilson's brain, nearly killing him. The stroke left him paralyzed on the left side, and it affected his speech. Most Americans, however, were not aware of how ill their president was.

▶ The Secret President

Woodrow Wilson was bedridden for several months. Although he continued to perform the duties of the president, it was Edith Wilson who decided what government business to bring to her husband.

At the time, there was no provision in the Constitution that dealt with a transfer of power if a sitting president became disabled. Some in Congress felt Wilson should step down. If he refused, they thought the matter should go before the Supreme Court. Others believed Congress should remove him. It was not until forty-eight years later that the question was answered. The Twenty-fifth Amendment, ratified in 1967, provides for the vice president to become acting president if the president becomes disabled and cannot perform his duties.

Woodrow Wilson did not step down, and rumors spread that it was Mrs. Wilson who was actually running the government.[8] Concerned about her husband's health and the effect that the stress of his office might have, she decided whom the president would see and what documents he would look at.[9] All other matters were handled by Wilson's cabinet members. Some called her the "secret president," and the "first woman to run the government."[10] In her book *My Memoir*, she said that her husband's doctors had encouraged her to do what she had done.[11] With Edith's help, Woodrow Wilson slowly recovered and was able to finish his term.

Final Months in Office

Wilson's final months in office brought both rewards and defeats. In November 1919 the Republican-dominated Senate rejected the Treaty of Versailles. That defeat shattered Wilson's dream for American participation in the League of Nations. If the United States had ratified the treaty, it would have been made a member of the League. It never became part of that organization. It was not until 1921, after Wilson had left office, that the United States finally signed a separate peace treaty with Germany.

In 1920, Woodrow Wilson was awarded the 1919 Nobel Peace Prize, for his efforts at securing peace after World War I. Also that year, the Nineteenth Amendment was ratified, finally giving American women (except American Indians) the right to vote.

Chapter 6 ▶

After the Presidency, 1921–1924

Woodrow Wilson never fully recovered from the stroke he suffered in 1919. He was too ill to run for a third term. In the 1920 election, Republican Warren G. Harding was elected president, and he took office on March 4, 1921. Woodrow and Edith Wilson left the White House and moved to their Washington, D.C., home. Wilson died

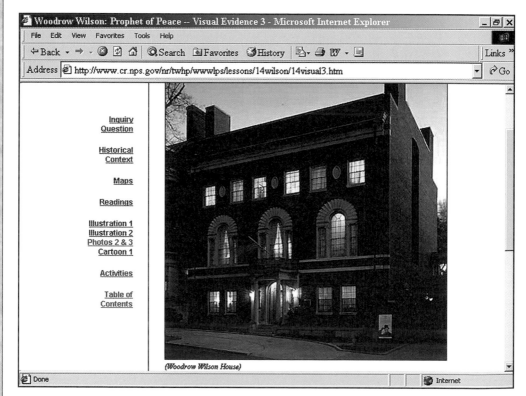

Woodrow Wilson: Prophet of Peace -- Visual Evidence 3 - Microsoft Internet Explorer

File Edit View Favorites Tools Help

← Back → ⊗ ⟳ ⌂ | ⬤ Search ⬛ Favorites ⬤ History | ⬔ ⬤ W ▾ ▤ | Links ⬝

Address ⬛ http://www.cr.nps.gov/nr/twhp/wwwlps/lessons/14wilson/14visual3.htm ▾ ⬁ Go

Inquiry
Question

Historical
Context

Maps

Readings

Illustration 1
Illustration 2
Photos 2 & 3
Cartoon 1

Activities

Table of
Contents

(Woodrow Wilson House)

Done Internet

In their final years, Woodrow and Edith Wilson lived in this Embassy Row town house in Washington, D.C. It is now a National Historic Landmark, open to the public.

there on February 3, 1924. He is buried in the National Cathedral, also in Washington.

▶ Wilson's Legacy

Historians consider Woodrow Wilson to have been one of our nation's greatest presidents. A poll of seventy-five historians ranked only George Washington, Abraham Lincoln, and Franklin Roosevelt above Wilson in importance.[1]

Wilson continued in the Progressive footsteps of his predecessors. When he took office, he was determined to see legislation passed that would further limit the powers of big business, and in that he was successful. He helped to pass antitrust laws that protected workers. With the Federal Reserve, he also created a new banking system. With Prohibition and Wilson's toleration of segregation, however, his administration took some large steps backward.

Wilson's foreign-policy decisions were some of the most challenging any president has had to make. After managing to keep the United States out of World War I for three years, Wilson finally asked Congress to declare war against Germany in 1917. After America entered the war, the tide turned and the Allies claimed victory less than two years later. Former Secretary of State Henry Kissinger has said that Woodrow Wilson's foreign policy helped shape United States foreign policy throughout the twentieth century.[2]

One of Wilson's greatest disappointments was Congress's rejection of the Treaty of Versailles, which was also a rejection of the League of Nations. But twenty-five years later, Wilson's dream of an international organization dedicated to peace and backed by the United States came into being. That organization was the United Nations, the successor to the League of Nations, and the United States was a charter member.

Chapter 1. Declaration of War

1. Edmund Ions, *Woodrow Wilson, the Politics of Peace and War* (New York: American Heritage Press, 1972), p. 72.

2. Brigham Young University, Harold B. Lee Library, World War I Digital Archives, *President Woodrow Wilson's address to Congress,* April 2, 1917, n.d., <http://www.lib.byu.edu/~rdh/wwi/1917/wilswarm.html> (May 6, 2002).

3. Ibid.

4. Ibid.

Chapter 2. Growing Up, 1856–1890

1. Edmund Ions, *Woodrow Wilson, the Politics of Peace and War* (New York: American Heritage Press, 1972), p. 112.

2. Grolier Online, *The American Presidency,* n.d., <http://gi.grolier.com/presidents/ea/bios/28pwils.html> (May 6, 2002).

3. Ions, p. 9.

4. PBS, *The American Experience—Woodrow Wilson,* n.d., <http://www.pbs.org/wgbh/amex/Wilson/portrait/wp_wilson.html> (May 6, 2002).

5. Ibid.

6. "Wilson's Fourteen Points," *American Treasures of the Library of Congress,* n.d., <http://www.loc.gov/exhibits/treasures/trm053.html> (May 6, 2002).

7. PBS, *The American Experience—Woodrow Wilson.*

8. Ohio Historical Society and Ohio State University, *Competing Visions for America,* n.d., <http://1912.history.ohio-state.edu/wilson.htm> (May 6, 2002).

Chapter 3. From Princeton to the White House, 1890–1913

1. PBS, *The American Experience—Woodrow Wilson,* n.d., <http://www.pbs.org/wgbh/amex/Wilson/portrait/wp_election.html> (May 6, 2002).

2. Ohio Historical Society and Ohio State University, *Competing Visions for America,* n.d., <http://1912.history.ohio-state.edu/debs.htm> (May 6, 2002).

Chapter 4. Wilson's First Administration, 1913–1917

1. Henry F. Graff, *The Presidents—A Reference History*, Second Edition (New York: Charles Scribner's and Sons, 1996), p. 366.

2. The White House, "State of the Union," n.d., <http://www.whitehouse.gov/stateoftheunion/history.html> (August 29, 2002).

3. Ohio Historical Society and Ohio State University, *Competing Visions for America*, n.d., <http://1912.history.ohio-state.edu/directdemocracy/> (May 6, 2002).

4. Kunhardt Productions/PBS, *The American President*, "The Visionary President—The Wilson Presidency: Domestic Affairs," n.d., <http://www.americanpresident.org/kotrain/courses/WW/WW_Domestic_Affairs.htm> (May 6, 2002).

5. PBS, *The American Experience—Woodrow Wilson*, n.d., <http://www.pbs.org/wgbh/amex/Wilson/portrait/wp_ellen.html> (May 6, 2002).

6. Tom Shachtman, *Edith & Woodrow* (New York: G.P. Putnam's Sons, 1918), p. 59.

7. The Jewish Museum, *The Jewish-American Hall of Fame—Louis D. Brandeis*, n.d., <http://amuseum.org/jahf/virtour/page12.html> (May 6, 2002).

8. Brandeis University Libraries, *Louis D. Brandeis*, n.d., <http://library.brandeis.edu/SpecialCollections/specialevents/Brandeis/zionism/zionism.html> (May 6, 2002).

9. Cleveland G. Allen, "The Negro and Politics," *The New York Times*, April 18, 1913, p. 10.

10. PBS, *The American Experience—Woodrow Wilson*, n.d., <http://www.pbs.org/wgbh/amex/wilson/portrait/wp_wilson.html> (May 6, 2002).

Chapter 5. Wilson's Second Administration, 1917–1921

1. David Kahn, *The Codebreakers: The Story of Secret Writing* (New York: Macmillan, 1967), p. 247.

2. "Text of President's Message to Congress," *The New York Times*, February 27, 1917, p. 1.

3. "Comment of Today's Newspapers on Sinking of American Ships," *The New York Times*, March 19, 1917, p. 1.

4. Brigham Young University, Harold B. Lee Library, World War I Digital Archives, *President Woodrow Wilson's Address to Congress*, April 2, 1917, <http://www.lib.byu.edu/~rdh/wwi/1917/wilswarm.html> (May 6, 2002).

5. Edmund Ions, *Woodrow Wilson, the Politics of Peace and War* (New York: American Heritage Press, 1972), p. 77.

6. Kunhardt Productions/PBS, *The American President*, "The Wilson Presidency: Domestic Affairs," n.d., <http://www.americanpresident.org/kotrain/courses/WW/WW_Domestic_Affairs.htm> (May 6, 2002).

7. Spartacus Educational, *Casualties of the First World War*, n.d., <http://www.spartacus.schoolnet.co.uk/FWWdeaths.htm> (May 6, 2002).

8. Ibid., p. 296.

9. Joseph Nathan Kane, *Facts About the Presidents* (New York: H. W. Wilson, 1993), p. 177.

10. The White House, *Past First Ladies—Edith Bolling Galt Wilson*, n.d., <http://www.whitehouse.gov/history/firstladies/ew28-2.html> (May 6, 2002).

11. Ibid.

Chapter 6. After the Presidency, 1921–1924

1. William A. DeGregorio, *The Complete Book of U.S. Presidents* (New York: Wings Books, 1997), p. 736.

2. Paul Dean, *Woodrow Wilson's Administration*, n.d., <http://www.geocities.com/Athens/2391/bio.htm> (May 6, 2002).

Brunelli, Carol and Ann Graham Gaines. *Woodrow Wilson: Our Twenty-Eighth President.* Chanhassen, Minn.: Child's World, Inc., 2001.

Collins, David R. and Richard G. Young, eds. *Woodrow Wilson: Twenty-Eighth President of the United States.* Ada, Okla.: Garrett Educational Corporation, 1989.

Esposito, David M. *The Legacy of Woodrow Wilson: American War Aims in World War I.* Westport, Conn.: Greenwood Publishing Group, Inc., 1996.

Ferrell, Robert H. *Woodrow Wilson and World War I, 1917–1921.* New York: HarperTrade, 1985.

Giblin, James Cross. *Women of Our Time—Edith Wilson: The Woman Who Ran the United States.* New York: Viking, 1992.

Krull, Kathleen. *Lives of the Presidents: Fame, Shame (and What the Neighbors Thought).* San Diego: Harcourt Brace & Co., 1998.

Leavell, J. Perry, Jr. *Woodrow Wilson.* New York: Chelsea House Publishers, 1987.

Lindop, Edmund. *Woodrow Wilson, Franklin D. Roosevelt, Harry S. Truman.* Brookfield, Conn.: Twenty-first Century Books, Inc., 1995.

Osinski, Alice. *Encyclopedia of Presidents: Woodrow Wilson.* Danbury, Conn.: Children's Press, 1989.

———. *Woodrow Wilson.* Danbury, Conn.: Children's Press, 1989.

Randolph, Sallie. *Woodrow Wilson.* New York: Walker & Company, 1992.

Schraff, Anne. *Woodrow Wilson.* Berkeley Heights, N.J.: Enslow Publishers, Inc., 1998.